The Rock-Art Files

Rock 'n Rhyme

I love rock art
And dainty rhymes
They cheer my heart
With such good times

T0380243

Contents

The Rock-Art Files

by

David and Rosina Shore

Dedication

To the many rock hounds
To those who have hit rock bottom
To those who are on the rocks
To those who are built upon the rock
To all who want a piece of the rock

Photography by

Howard J. White

Prelude

O come, let us sing unto the Lord: let us make a joyful noise to the rock of our salvation

Psalm 95:1

Foreword – The Rocky Road

The road leading up to the formation of "The Rock-Art Files" has been rather rocky. This concrete idea came to us near Boulder City in the Rocky Mountains. It hit us like a ton of bricks. At first we were petrified. Our business firm was on the rocks, our finances had hit rock bottom and we were really up against a stone wall.

To undertake such a heavy project some thought we were off our rocker. But as we got the stone rolling the way became crystal clear and our hopes began to sky rocket. After all, America was born at Plymouth Rock and Rockefeller was Vice-President. This generation loves hard rock and the Rolling Stones. Rock Hudson is famous in Movieland and Rockford is popular on television. So rock 'n rhyme seemed to be the solid thing to do. It could become the cornerstone in building our future.

Rock was the big thing in the Stone Age and today we are still after a piece of the rock. in fact we have become so fond of rocks that we make little pets out of them. This unusual affinity for pet pebbles could serve as a stepping stone to generate wide-spread interest in "The Rock-Art Files."

Introduction – Pleasant Stones

We scanned river beds and hills
For these characters in stone
And one of our greatest thrills
Was giving them flesh and bone
We spent many pleasant hours
With brush and pen, paint and glue
And decorating with f lowers
Sceneries of rainbow hue
All the animals and birds
Are saying to you and me
Many things in simple words
And humming a melody
There's Humpty and Santa Claus
Herbie and Red Riding Hood
A lion with gentle paws
And a moon made out of wood
A giant called Jolly Green
And three Birds of Paradise
The Ship of Fools can be seen
And a band of fiddling mice
A war between King and Kong
An Aku 'neath a palm tree
Two lovers singing a song
And a real live rock ducky
Many others join the f un
Rolling high on rock'n rhyme
They've found a place in the sun
And brightened our world of time

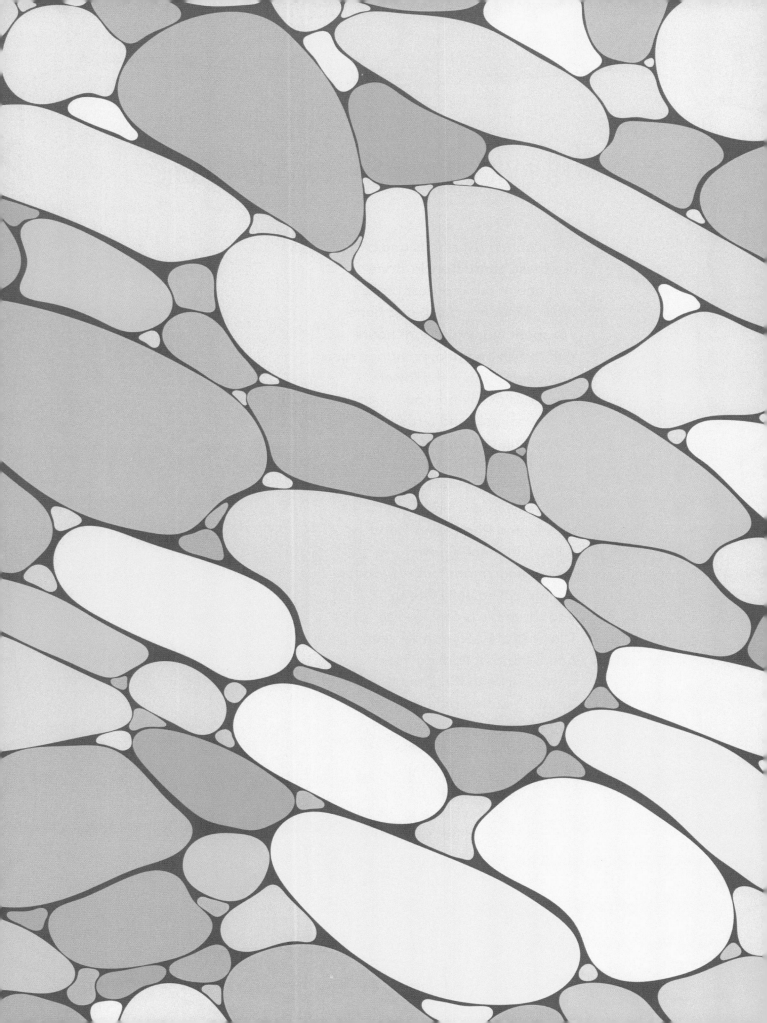

Pop Rock and the Precious Stones

This picture was taken up against a stone wall which is where we were when we started this heavy project. A back injury, incurred as a sheetrocker, kept Pop home f or over three years. The most painful part was when Pop was hospitalized for a kidney stone. Mom was a pearl during this difficult period, being the keystone of the operation.

We were stone-broke and needed a creative project to keep us busy. So working on the book was like killing two birds with one stone. We put our noses to the grindstone and became avid rock hounds. We scanned the valley from Red Rock Canyon to the rocky slopes of Sunrise Mountain. We left no stone unturned. Mom had experience from France in sculpture and painting. Pop tried his hand at writing and publishing the book. Mom did all the illustrations and the photography was done by a friend of ours, Howard White.

The children were jewels in helping with the household chores. They took turns rocking the baby to sleep. They were excited to see all the animals and birds come to life. Some of the children made creations of their own which are shown in the Pebble Pages.

The whole project has been a milestone in our lives. It turned out to be a family affair and we hope it will be enjoyed by all.

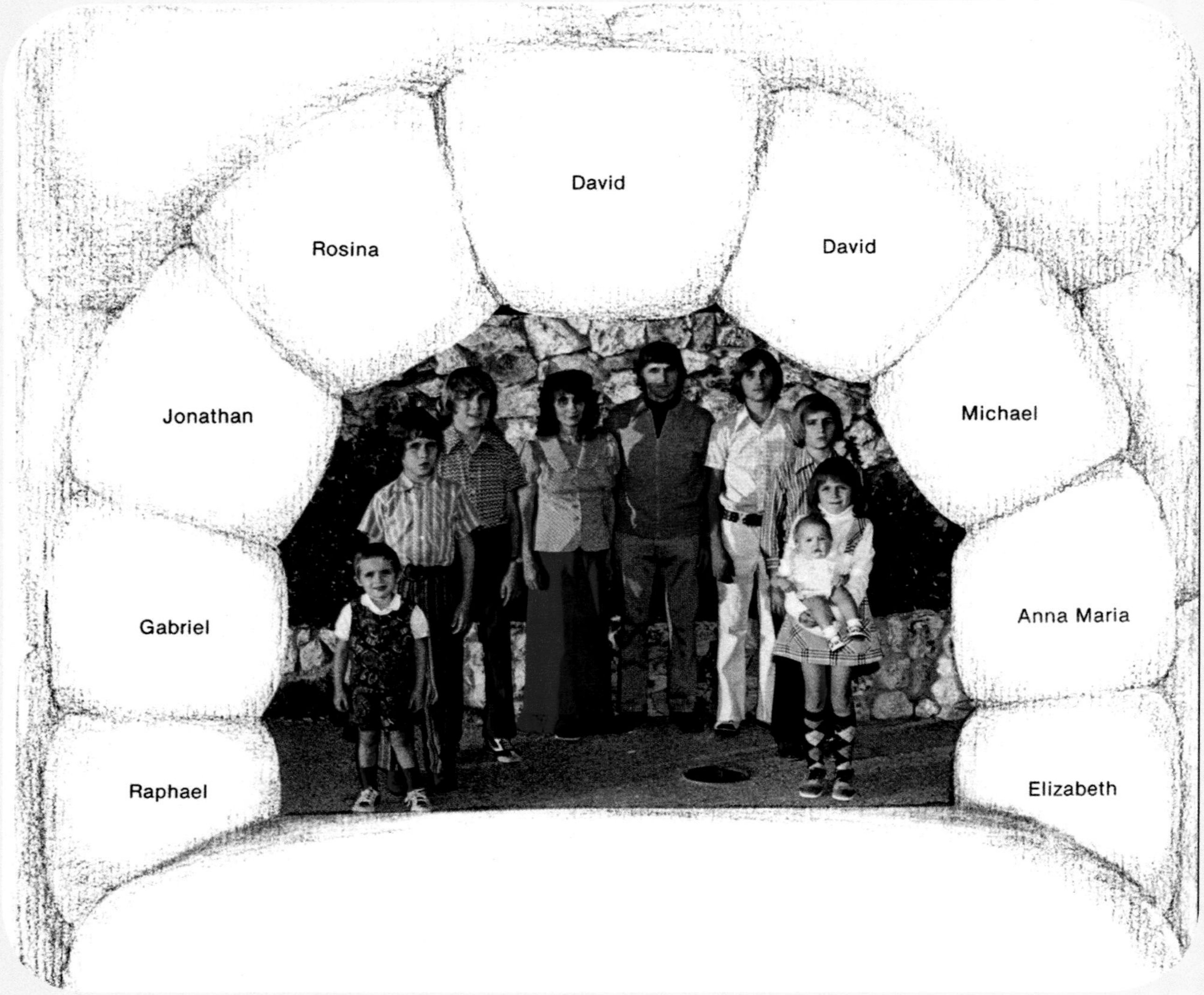
David
Rosina
David
Jonathan
Michael
Gabriel
Anna Maria
Raphael
Elizabeth

The SH "ore" Rock Group

We were up against a stone wall
And it was hard to make ends meet
The road was rocky f or us all
But now we hope its easy street

Boulder Bulletin

Rocks tell us many stories. We used this abundant material to tell us even more stories. This project began in 1974 as a pastime. Sculpture, painting and poetry were combined to make up "The Rock-Art Files." We started with small characters but realized many interesting subjects could be made with larger rocks. Each creation was designed to tell a story which is expressed in a short rhyme. The possibilities of rock 'n rhyme fascinated us and we felt it would have universal appeal for all ages.

Sandy and Rocky Stoneman were our first creation. Their wheat is being stoneground in crockery. The slumped over Mexican is slumpstone. The big foot of the Jolly Green Giant is a foot long. The monster Kong is porous imitation rock representing evil. Ultra King, who represents good, is immovable as the Rock of Ages. The sounding of the Liberty Bell rocked the world. The flags are pieces of flagstone. Captain Stone is a goldbricker. Red Riding Hood's basket and contents are made out of bread dough. Adolph the little bad wolf is a good beef hip bone. There is a stonefly above Kermit the frog. The Abominable Snowman could be an old fossil. The hillbillies are rhinestone cowboys. They got stoned on rock 'n rye.

Flopper is a stone-fish and the flappers are rocklings. The stonechats are of the thrush family. They make a peculiar sound like two stones being struck together. One of the Mice Rock Group is a rolling stone. The Birds of Paradise are surrounded by rock flowers. The craggy height is a mountain of loadstone.

When we first put Humpty Dumpty on the stone wall, he fell off but it was a good break because he was still in one piece. The moon is a slab of driftwood set against the curtains of heaven. Herbie the Love Bug and all his passengers are rock. The tires on the Volks are Firestone. The Sheriff is a keystone cop. Michael's Mommy made my Mummy. Within a stone's throw is the little pyramid. It represents the great one which is made of limestone and granite.

We called the camel Humphrey because he doesn't have a hump. The Rock Ducky won't float but if placed beside the tub he makes a good sitting duck. Big Bird is the biggy and the heaviest of all. This completes the Boulder Bulletin except for the fact that we have fallen in love with all of these priceless gems.

The Featherstone Family

There once was a family that
Were neither flesh or bone
We put a feather in their hat
And called them Featherstone
Our boy Flint and pet Pebbles too
Are a part of this happy through
They will lead us all the way through
And make us feel that we belong

America

The emblems of our liberty
No sweeter land could ever be
Gold arrows point the way on high
Our eagle soaring in the sky

The Moonstones

The moon is sailing in the sky
And all her creatures 'round her fly
The fiddling cat and jumping cow
A cute little dish and doggie's bow

A mouse is roaring on her nose
The silver spoon on tippy toes
T'is all a dream in fantasy
But oh so real to kids and me

Humpty Dumpty

A good old egg am I
Fit for a king to fry
The birds sing in the trees
While I sit in the breeze
Afraid to fall and cry I

The Desert Hat

The lowly sombrero
Is worn by old Zorro
O'er the desert he cries
Riding as the crow flies

Speedy Gonzales

After the fiesta
Comes the siesta
And it'll be mañana
When I eat that banana

Aku

Aku are we
'Neath the palm tree
Aku, Aku
You're all kuku

Mervin and Myrtle

Guess you know
We're a little slow
But we get there
With time to spare
And we don't care
To race a hare

Felix

Would you believe this here cat
Could really eat all there that
I've licked the can of garbage clean
And now my belly can be seen

Herbie

What we have here folks
Is a far out Volks
The people inside
Are taking a ride
On dirt and gravel
Herbie will travel
And when there's a cop
He'll come to a stop

The Owl and The Pussycat

The Owl and the Pussycat on the go go
One gives a hoot and the other a row row
Up and down the river like a yo yo
But don't rock the boat 'cause that's a no no

The Wise Old Owl

Listen to Olie the wise old owl
Whoo is the smartest of all the fowl
You younger ones have alot to learn
What really makes this pretty world turn

Love, Peace, Joy

Divine beauty arrayed as one
In legend fly above the sun
Like rainbow hues in summer skies
Delightful birds of Paradise

Rock and Raquel

My lover is going away
And leaving me alone to stay
But while we are here in the park
We whisper sweet words in the dark
The birds will stop singing tomorrow
And my heart will be filled with sorrow
But our love is true and always near
And when he returns I'll still be here

Joe and Judy

A little kiss
How sweet it iss!
And when we sing
Our voices ring

The Stonechats

I love the Spring
When stonechats sing
And roses bloom
On winter's tomb

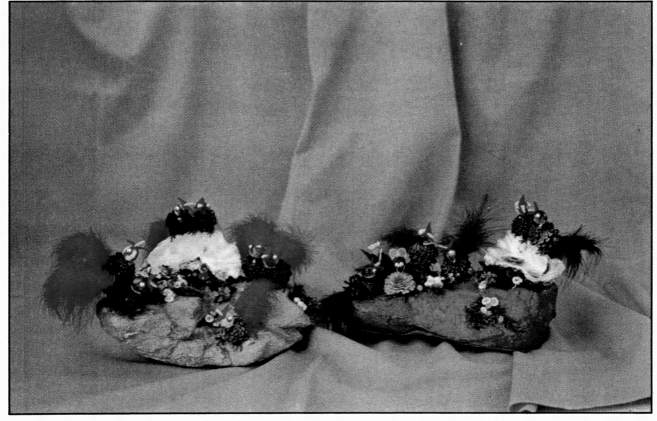

Hold That Tiger

We've been used in many a tale
But there is one that's really rank
Hold that tiger by the tail
And put it in your gas tank

Bigfoot

I've planted my giant green toes
In the valley of the ho hoes
Where jolly peas around me grow
And there's no need for big scarecrow

Mummy

Mommy made my mummy
And her little dummy
Wrapped up by her tummy
And in a stone nearby
Is the pyramid eye
Who watches as they die
Tut-tutsie goodbye

Molly and Dolly

One summer morn
In a field of corn
Dolly was born

Shelly

Slowly and steadily I creep
While the hare is fast asleep
I sure wish that I could hurdle
But I am just a turtle

Fred and Barney

We were the rage
On the front page
Of the Stone Age

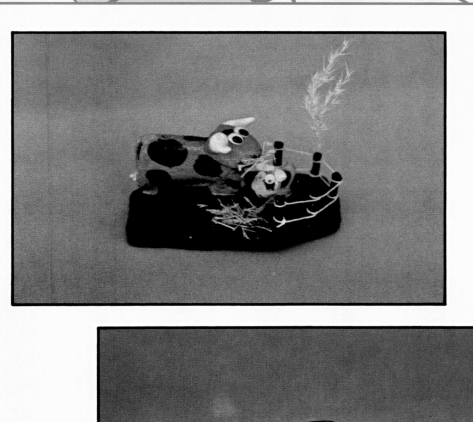

The Mice Rock Group

Three stone-blind mice are fiddling around
Two in the air and one on the ground
They're playing Kitty's favorite tune
And stars are dancing around the moon

Daffy

Boy! I sure do feel lucky
To have a real rock ducky
I know he doesn't float or swim
But I just like to look at him

Francis

You may have heard
A stubborn word
But that's absurd
I'm not even lazy
And the reason I look crazy
Is from pushing up the daisy

Jude and Alfie

When you cry for help
We come with a yelp
We run to our man
As fast as we can

Pinky and Kitty

The whole kit 'n caboodle
Is a kitten 'n French Poodle
Inky Pinky parlez-vous?
Oui Madame, how about you?

The Rock Garden

I spend my hours
Among rock flowers
Where lilies mushroom
And morning glories bloom

Rock-a-Bye Baby

Rock-a-bye my baby love
Sleep in peace throughout the night
Dream of angels from above
Who keep watch till morning light

Captain Stone

Alright! dibby up you guys
Or I'll get you between the eyes
Give me all your gold and loot
And hurry up before I shoot

The Piggy Bank Tale

These little piggies went to the stock market
On the Wall Street of New York
To bring home the bacon they tried to loan shark it
But only brought ham and pork
And caught the swine flu
From living high on the hog

Rocco

I roam the mountains capped with snow
Sometimes I take a stroll below
My face is cloaked in mystery
'Cause it's the worst in history

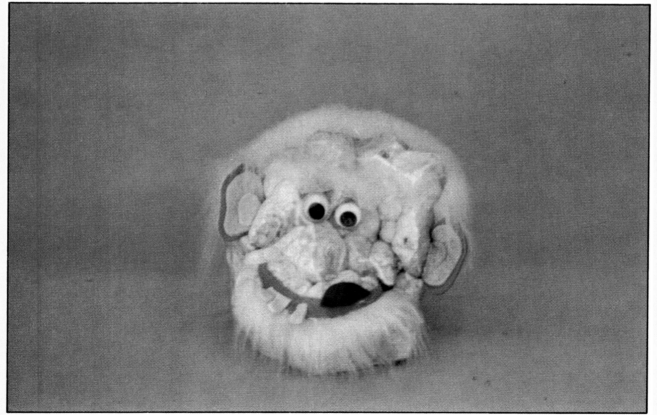

Sandy and Rocky Stoneman

Said he, "It's plain to see
She's too much for me
I think I'll rest awhile
And let her work the pile."

Jackstone and the Rocking Horse

We should pull together as a team
For we belong to the working class
It's not as easy as it may seem
Because one of us is a jackass

The Crocketts

Let's go to the party later
You slimy green alligator
There's a place in the muggy swamp
Where I'd rather frolic and romp
And dry up my crocodile tears

Henrietta

I may be a bit overweight
But that's the way all hippos rate
We love to lay around all day
And make big waves in Hippo Bay

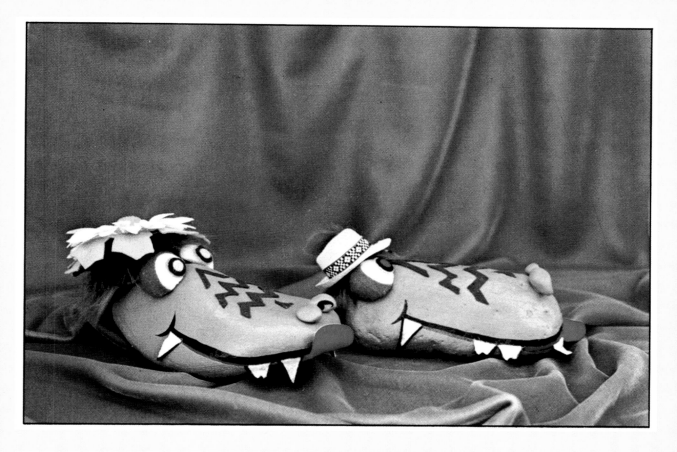

Butch

I like to be heard but not seen
'Cause I'm ugly and a bit mean
But if you want a good watch dog
I'm better than a big fat hog

Henny Penny and the Spring Chickens

What's the matter little chick?
If you don't eat you'll get sick
So hop right down and pick the ground
'Cause they sell fryers by the pound

Zan, Zane and Zany

Zan and Zane of the jungle clan
Date way back to primitive man
Their little friend Zany the chump
Is sweeter than a sugar lump
In those days life was really slow
And woman had a ways to go

Wild West

The cowboy's at rest
In the wild wild west
But the fight goes on
Till the new day dawn

The Cuckoo monster

A good little monster am I
As I horse around in the sky
But when I get a bit too high
My fiery mouth gets awful dry
Now Cuckoo Monster say goodbye

Red Cloud and Gentle Rain

I Indian Brave and she my Squaw
I big chief but she big mama
We make good home in large teepee
She work hard while I go sleepy

Stony Stan and Gravel Gertie

Your raggedy mop
A clock would stop
Once you were fair
With lovelier hair
Upon your top

The Three Little Nuts

We are three little nuts
Who are in three big ruts
The squirrel is on the prowl
And that man with a growl
Wants us stored in their huts

The Micekitears

Did you ever see such a sight
As a whole bunch of mice at night
They nibble on cheese
While Kitty's at ease
And hope they won't get in a fight

Humphrey

I tote my load to distant lands
Across the arid desert sands
And when my mouth is hot and dry
My humps do all my needs supply

Geraldine

Geraldine among the trees
Standing tall up in the breeze
Her head is now a little low
Nibbling shamrock wouldn't you know

Droopy and Spot

Don't be a hog
You lucky dog
Be fair and square
And take your share

Bugs

Hey there! what's up Doc?
Did ya see my rock?
Now grin and bear it
That's a raw carrot

Donald

I'm a lame duck
And you're bad luck
So get off' a me
You bumbling bee

Cheetah

We made a monkey out of you
And left you free to do your thing
Jumping down is easy to do
But harder is the upward swing

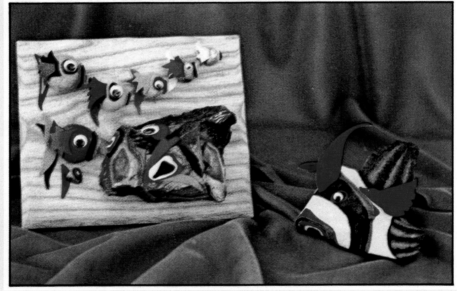

Mina Bird

From the Pelican was heard
"Is'a that'a you'a bird?"
The wise owl hooted this word
"Yessuh, that's a Mina Bird"

Flopper and the Flappers

A school of fish
Have made a wish
Let's swim and play
In school today

Jaws

Should you go for a dip
And you hear two buzz saws
You'd better let her rip
'Cause it's bound to be Jaws

Flint and Pebbles

We're true rock hounds
On crag and shale
And making rounds
O'er hill and dale

We're filing through
The stony piles
That all may view
The Rock-Art Files

Liberty Ship

Sailing out to open sea
Is the good ship Liberty
Guided by a mighty hand
Leading to the promised land

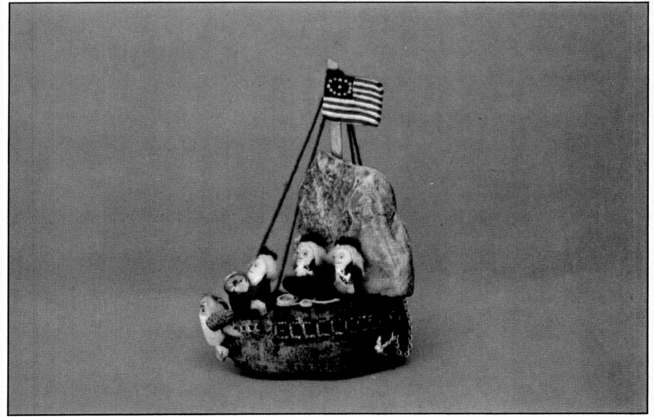

Bozo

Clowning around is my favorite thing
As I laugh and cry and crazily sing
The kiddies delight to my funny ways
And happy am I to brighten their days
Now that went over like a rock balloon

Red and Adolph

Oh! Oh! there's Adolph
The little bad wolf
That's why Mommy said
"Take care darling Red."

Says Adolph in the wood
"Mmm that sure looks good
I'll bet she's on her way
To Grandma's house, Olay!"

Proud Bird with a Golden Tale

I'm a proud peacock
With a stony stare
And no other rock
Can even compare

Sadie and Sarge

We hold a ball upon our nose
And under water wag our toes
In summer time we make a show
We nod our head and then we blow

Kermit

Looking up with glassy eyes
Kermit's busy chasing flies
Now and then you hear a croak
As he jumps beneath the oak

Stonewall and Rockney

Way back in them thar hills
Thar are some whiskey stills
That's whar we had our thrills
And got stoned to the gills

Porgy and Bess

Porgy and Bess of noble birth
Hai I from the warmer parts of earth
Their kingdom is a happy one
With children playing in the sun

A royal feast has been proclaimed
A special day for Bess is named
Porgy is clad in kingly dress
For this is the day he says, YES!

Moby and the Gladstones

Mermaids are not for real you know
In ancient myth it tells us so
But Moby used to roam the seas
In search of creatures just like these

Nick and Martha

Here comes Mr. and Mrs. Santa Claus
Jolliest of all the papas and mamas
Their huge sack is filled with goodies and toys
Warming the hearts of little girls and boys

Martha sure is a merry old soul
She loves to help Nick at the cold North Pole
Wrapping all the gifts for next Christmas night
When kind hearts again look up in delight

Porky, Peggy and the Penguiunees

Porky and Peggy from Penguin Isle
Strutting on ice with their Penguinees
All decked out in tuxedo style
Proudly they show off their bambinis

Big Bird and Little Bird

A chip off the block
All made out of rock
But just add a word
And there is Big Bird

His cute little friend
Is true to the end
Witty and alert
Like Ernie with Bert

The Good Fairy and the Wicked Witch

When the moon is high
In the Autumn sky
The witch can be seen
Howling, "Hallowe'en!"

But on Christmas night
When the stars are bright
The Good Fairy sings
And joy to all brings

Turkey Lurkey

I see you turkey in the straw
Strutting along with heavy feet
With rocks and gravel in your craw
You just gotta be hard to eat

Sammy

Sammy is a sweet little lamb
Whiter than all the other ram
He follows the shepherd where'er he goes
His gentle nature within him glows

Polly

Polly's not a quacker
But she really talks
Polly wants a cracker
With scotch on the rocks

Frosty

Frosty sure is fun to make
Even though his nose is fake
Every winter he comes to town
And never does he wear a frown
With beaming grin from ear to ear
He wishes all a Happy New Year

Ship of Fools

There brews a storm way up ahead
And in that way we're being led
There is still time to turn aside
But who can guide the ship in stride

We hope the storm will go away
For we have things to do today
So eat and drink and merry be
And time will tell what we shall see

Star War

Ultra King battles monstrous Kong
An unseen war between right and wrong
But the almighty forces of good
Shall triumph among earth's brotherhood

Rock Around The Clock

We've rolled and rocked around the clock
And passed the time with lots of talk
But the hour has come to take stock
For we are waiting for THE ROCK

For He shall come to reign as King
And peace in every heart will bring
The rocks and hills his praises sing
And every day be thanksgiving

The Lamb and The Lion

The lamb and the lion
Are dwelling side by side
Friends at last in Zion
Where peace and love abide

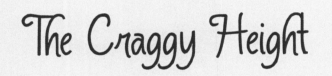

The Craggy Height

We've reached at last the mountain top
As evening shadows fall
The time has come for us to stop
So thanks for comin' y'all

Headstone and Bedlock

Yes! I've been down that rocky road
And scaled the craggy heights alone
I've left behind my heavy load
And now I rest beneath a stone

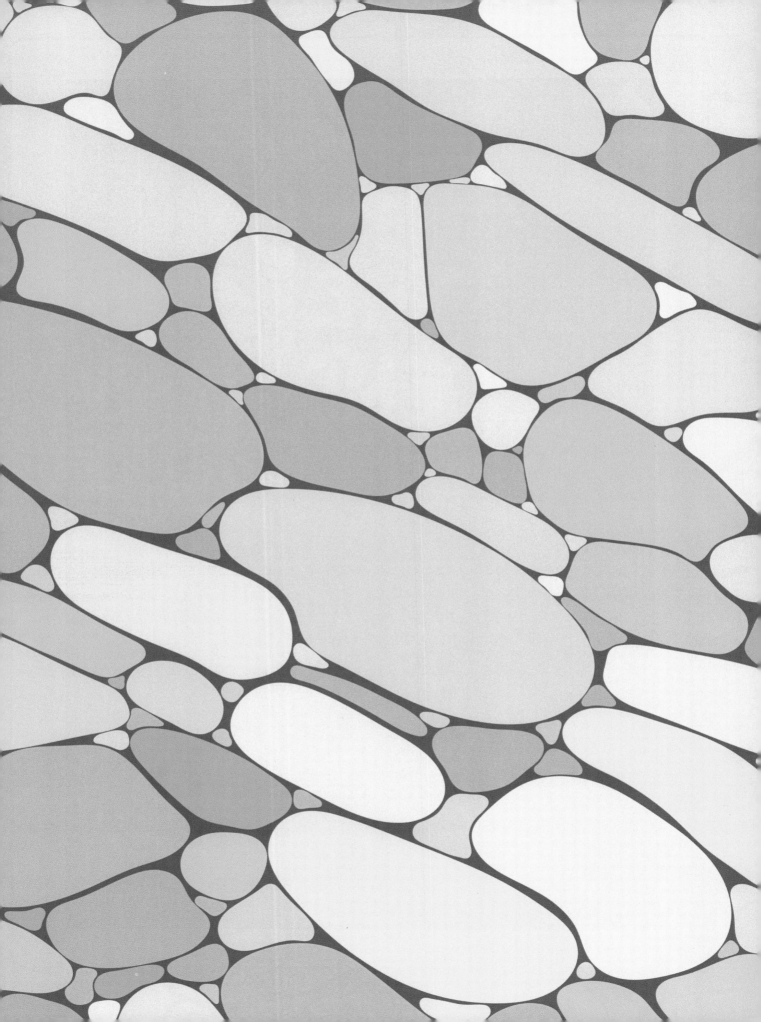

Epilogue

*For there is none holy
as the Lord: for there
is none beside thee:
neither is there any
rock like our God.*

1 Samuel 2:2

Printed in the United States
by Baker & Taylor Publisher Services